A Chris Adventure Book

Copyright © 2017 by J. Lew

Little Ranch Hands
By J. Lew

Printed in the United States of America

ISBN 9781946806086

All rights reserved solely by the author. No part of this book may be reproduced or transmitted in any form or by any means without the written permission from the author.

www.jlew-books.com

Chris and his family have just arrived at their grandparents' ranch. They grab their luggage from the van and run onto the porch where Mimi and Pape' are waiting.

"It's so nice to see you grandkids!" greet Mimi and Pape'.

Chris and his siblings get lots of hugs and kisses.

After dinner, Chris and Danny rush to their room. The two of them will sleep in bunk beds.

Toni is in her room with Candie, reading a book until she falls asleep.

After breakfast, everyone waves goodbye to David and Tiffani, the children's parents.

"We will miss you!" says Chris.

"We sure will!" add Danny and Toni.

David and Tiffani wave at the kids. "We'll see you soon," they say.

Toni, Danny, and Chris are anxious to see the horses, Maximus and Snowy. The children feed them hay and pilled apples.

"I hope you like your snack!" Toni says to Snowy.

The kids' first day on the ranch is full of fun and games. Pape' takes the children out on the range to see the cattle and drop off some hay from the back of his truck.

The day is long and lots of fun. Toni, Danny, and Chris are inside the corral giving the horses water and hay before they go back to the house.

The next day, Chris and his family enjoy a nice Sunday morning at church. Chris loves to sing along with everybody. Sometimes he sings a little off-key, but he loves the choir all the same.

It's Monday morning and everyone is up before sunrise. Chris is tired and doesn't want to get out of bed.

"It's too early," he whines. "It's still nighttime."

While Toni and Danny collect fresh eggs, Chris chases the chickens. Candie and Rowdy bark at them from outside the chicken fence.

Pape' is showing the children how he and Mimi milked the cows before they used milking machines. Danny and Chris wait their turn while Toni milks one of the cows.

After they milk the cows, the children clean the stalls.

"This is fun," Chris says cheerfully.

Toni, Danny, and Chris make butter the old-fashioned way. They churn the cream until it is soft and smooth.

Toni, Danny, and Chris are very tired the next day. It is hot outside, so Mimi lets them splash around in the pool. The children enjoy their time in the water.

Today Chris, Toni, and Danny are in the field pouring corn for the deer and turkeys that roam the ranch. The animals are hungry.

The children spend the next day with Pape' out on the range. They are going out to repair some fence posts that one of the bulls pushed over.

Later in the week, they work in the garden with Mimi. They pick carrots, beets, and peas while Mimi shows them how to dig up potatoes.

Danny is cutting the front lawn for Pape'. Chris and Toni are watching from the porch.

"Toni, I wish I were older so we could take turns mowing the yard like Danny," Chris whispers to his sister.

"Someday you'll be old enough," Toni assures him.

Mimi and Toni are in the kitchen. Toni is helping her grandmother bake apple pies.
"It smells really good in here," say Danny and Chris. "Mmm."
The two brothers sniff the air and cannot wait to dig into the pie.

After a long, hard day, Mimi wants to have a picnic by the pond. Toni, Danny, and Chris are tired, but they love running around the water. The siblings feed the ducks and watch them swim.

Pape' is splitting logs with help from Toni, Danny, and Chris. They all take turns pulling the handle to split the logs. Chris pulls the handle and the cutter splits the log into two pieces.

The next morning, the children and Pape' enjoy a horseback ride around the ranch.

"This is peaceful," says Toni.

"I like it a lot," adds Chris.

Danny nods in agreement.

Before their visit comes to an end, Chris, Toni, and Danny learn archery on the ranch. The activity is not as easy as it looks.

Before they know it, Chris, Toni, Danny, and Candie are going home. Everybody exchanges hugs and says goodbye.

"Goodbye, Mimi and Pape'!" the children say. "Goodbye, Rowdy! We will miss you."

"We will miss you too," their grandparents reply.

LITTLE RANCH HANDS

A Chris Adventure Book

More books by J. Lew
I'm Not Afraid of the Dark
Sunken Treasures

Look for more of Chris Adventure Books!

Thanks
J. Lew

www.ingramcontent.com/pod-product-compliance
Lightning Source LLC
Chambersburg PA
CBHW081358080526
44588CB00016B/2539